AF228537

WHY IS THE OCEAN SALTY?

by Debbie Vilardi

Cody Koala

An Imprint of Pop!

popbooksonline.com

abdobooks.com
Published by Pop!, a division of ABDO, PO Box 398166, Minneapolis, Minnesota 55439. Copyright © 2019 by POP, LLC. International copyrights reserved in all countries. No part of this book may be reproduced in any form without written permission from the publisher. Pop!™ is a trademark and logo of POP, LLC.

Printed in the United States of America, North Mankato, Minnesota

092018
012019

THIS BOOK CONTAINS RECYCLED MATERIALS

Cover Photo: iStockphoto
Interior Photos: iStockphoto, 1, 5 (bottom left), 9, 10, 11, 20–21; Shutterstock Images, 5 (top), 5 (bottom right), 6, 13, 15, 17, 18

Editor: Meg Gaertner
Series Designer: Laura Mitchell

Library of Congress Control Number: 2018950148
Publisher's Cataloging-in-Publication Data
Names: Vilardi, Debbie, author.
Title: Why is the ocean salty? / by Debbie Vilardi.
Description: Minneapolis, Minnesota : Pop!, 2019 | Series: Science questions | Includes online resources and index.
Identifiers: ISBN 9781532162190 (lib. bdg.) | ISBN 9781641855907 (pbk) | ISBN 9781532163258 (ebook)
Subjects: LCSH: Ocean--Juvenile literature. | Seawater--Juvenile literature. | Salinity--Juvenile literature. | Children's questions and answers--Juvenile literature.
Classification: DDC 500--dc23

Hello! My name is

Cody Koala

Pop open this book and you'll find QR codes like this one, loaded with information, so you can learn even more!

Scan this code* and others like it while you read, or visit the website below to make this book pop.

popbooksonline.com/ocean-salty

*Scanning QR codes requires a web-enabled smart device with a QR code reader app and a camera.

Table of Contents

Chapter 1

Oceans

Oceans are large bodies of water. They cover most of Earth's surface. There are five named oceans. They are all connected.

Watch a video here!

Ocean water is not safe for drinking. It contains too many **minerals**. Some of these minerals are salts. That is why ocean water is also called salt water.

The five oceans are the Atlantic, Pacific, Indian, Arctic, and Southern, or Antarctic, Oceans.

Chapter 2

Water Power

Rivers **erode** the rocks they move through. Minerals from rocks **dissolve** in the river water. Rivers carry these minerals to the oceans.

Learn more here!

Rainwater also washes minerals into the ocean. Melting ice brings minerals to the ocean too.

Some parts of the ocean
receive more of this **runoff**.
These areas are saltier.

Chapter 3

Evaporation

The sun heats the earth.

Water **evaporates** as

temperatures rise.

But minerals do not.

Learn more here!

The same amount of minerals is dissolved in less water. That part of the ocean becomes saltier.

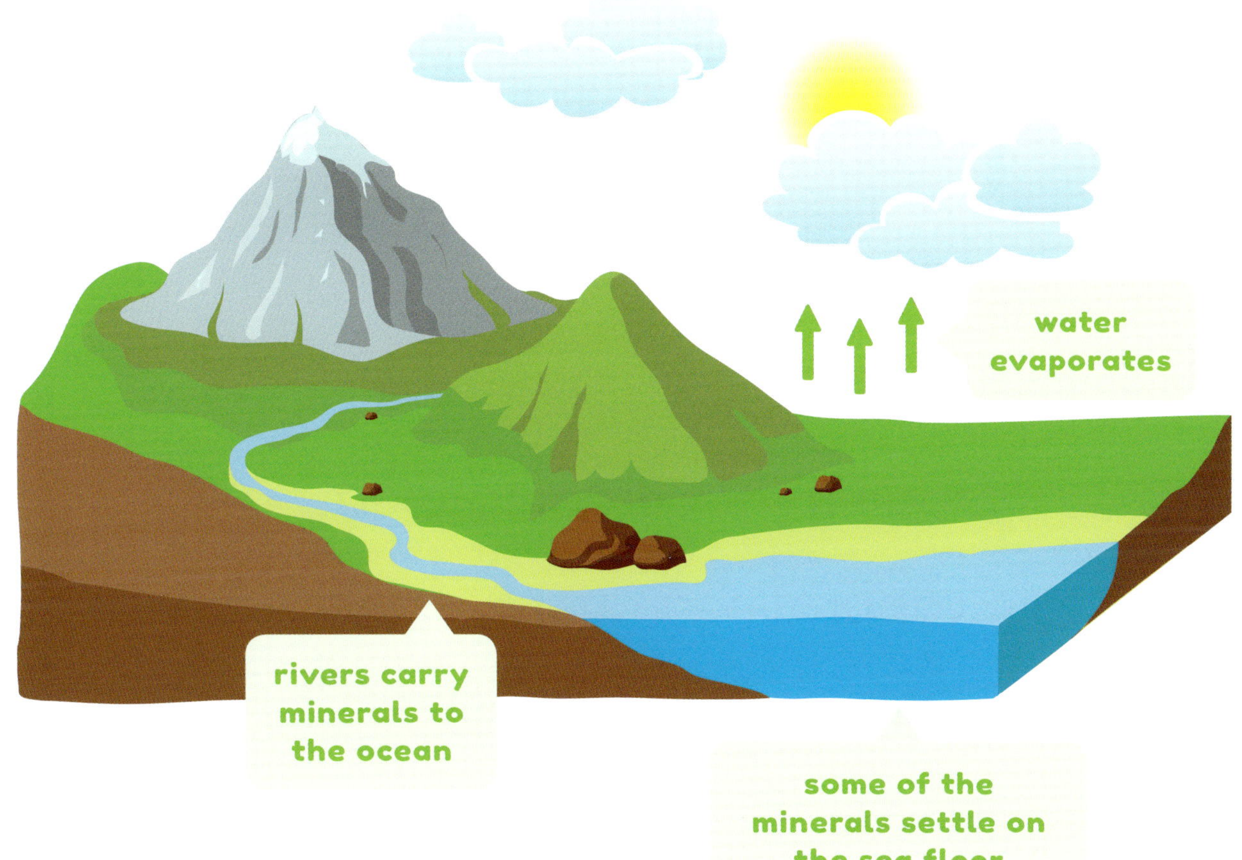

water evaporates
rivers carry minerals to the ocean
some of the minerals settle on the sea floor

Chapter 4

Salinity

The salty oceans were
created a long time ago.
Eroding rock created them.
Evaporating water helped.

Complete an
activity here!

Minerals flow into the ocean. But they leave the ocean too. Some minerals sink to the ocean floor. Other minerals are used by ocean animals.

Salts enter and leave the ocean. The overall change in **salinity** levels is very tiny.

Ocean salinity has not
changed much for millions
of years.

Making Connections

Text-to-Self

Have you ever been to the ocean? If yes, what did you think? If no, would you like to? Why or why not?

Text-to-Text

Have you read other books about the ocean? What new thing did you learn?

Text-to-World

Why do you think ocean water is not safe for drinking?

Glossary

dissolve – to become part of a liquid such as water.

erode – to slowly wear away because of water or some other natural force.

evaporate – to change from a liquid into a gas.

mineral – a substance naturally formed in the ground that is neither a plant nor an animal.

runoff – water and the substances dissolved in it draining from the land into the ocean.

salinity – a measure of the salt in a substance.

Index

Online Resources

popbooksonline.com

Thanks for reading this Cody Koala book!

Scan this code* and others like it in this book, or visit the website below to make this book pop!

popbooksonline.com/ocean-salty

*Scanning QR codes requires a web-enabled smart device with a QR code reader app and a camera.